THE FISHER KING
AND THE
HANDLESS MAIDEN

Also by Robert A. Johnson

He: Understanding Masculine Psychology

She: Understanding Feminine Psychology

*We: Understanding the Psychology of
Romantic Love*

*Inner Work: Using Dreams and Active Imagination
for Personal Growth*

Ecstasy: Understanding the Psychology of Joy

Femininity Lost and Regained

*Transformation: Understanding the Three Levels
of Masculine Consciousness*

*Owning Your Own Shadow: Understanding the
Dark Side of the Psyche*

The Fisher King
and the
Handless Maiden

*Understanding the Wounded Feeling Function
in Masculine and Feminine Psychology*

ROBERT A. JOHNSON

HarperSanFrancisco
A Division of HarperCollinsPublishers

FIRST EDITION

Library of Congress Cataloging-in-Publication Data

Johnson, Robert A.
    The fisher king and the handless maiden : understanding
the wounded feeling function in masculine and feminine
psychology /   Robert A. Johnson. — 1st ed.
     p. cm.
    ISBN 0–06–250647–1 (cloth : alk. paper).
    ISBN 0–06–250648–x (pbk. : alk. paper).
    ISBN 0–06–250918–7 (intl. pbk. : alk. paper)
    1. Masculinity (Psychology)   2. Femininity (Psychology)
I. Title.
BF175.5.M37J64   1993   92–53213
155.3—dc20   CIP

93 94 95 96 97 ❖ RRD(H) 10 9 8 7 6 5 4 3 2 1

This edition is printed on acid-free paper that meets the American National Standards Institute Z39.48 Standard.

CONTENTS

The Fisher King
and the
Handless Maiden

INTRODUCTION

THIS BOOK IS ABOUT OUR wounded feeling function, probably the most common and painful wound which occurs in our Western world. It is very dangerous when a wound is so common in a culture that hardly anyone knows that there is a problem. There is general discontent with our way of life but almost no one knows specifically where to look for its origin.

Thinking is that cool faculty which brings clarity and objectivity—but provides no valuing; sensation describes the physical world—but provides no valuing; intuition suggests a wide range of possibilities—but provides no valuing. Only feeling brings a sense of value and worth; indeed, this is its chief function. Without feeling there is no value judgment. To lose one's feeling function is thus to lose one of the most precious human faculties, perhaps the one that makes us most human. We can understand the term *feeling* more accurately if we define it as the capacity to value or to give worth to something. People who have a finely differentiated feeling function bring grace and good feeling with them; one feels valuable in their presence.

The feeling function is a casualty of our modern way of life. To search out the loss—or woundedness—of this most valuable faculty is the task of our book.

The wounded feeling function is so common in our Western world that one must completely leave this civilization to gain insight into the problem. America reveals some of its specific characteristics only when viewed from Europe; our Western world reveals some of its secrets only when viewed from the East. It was not until I had lived in India for some time that I began to discover the degree of the wounding of our feeling function.

The very term *feeling* is itself ambiguous, an orphan word. Its true meaning has not quite differentiated itself from its tactile origins. It derives from the verb *to feel* in its tactile sense. Our use of the word *feeling* is made to describe much more subtle realms. The act of valuing has no dignified term of its own and is still tied by an unseen umbilical cord to the realm of sensation. Little wonder that strong feeling is unconsciously tied to some physical act that we think should give expression to it. Of course, one may make sublime expression of feeling by a physical act, but feeling should not be unconsciously tied to the physical realm. *Feeling* is one of the wonderful, terrible, ambiguous words that contribute so much to our confusion.

A movement is afoot to expunge some of the great words of our language—such as *God, freedom, democracy,* and *love*—that have become so global in their associations that they mean nothing in practicality. *Feeling* might top the list. I don't know what we would put in their place—perhaps a dozen words of more differentiated meaning for each one—but we could at least start afresh. My good friend John Sanford, a Jungian analyst and Episcopal priest, shocks people who ask him if he believes in God by replying, "Do you mean Jaweh, Jehovah, The Elohim, or the God of the New Testament?"

Introduction

To have clarity in one's question is half the way to getting an intelligent answer.

THE VOCABULARY OF FEELING

The first difficulty we meet in discussing anything concerning the feeling function is that we have no adequate vocabulary to use. Where there is no terminology, there is no consciousness. A poverty-stricken vocabulary for any subject is an immediate admission that the subject is inferior or depreciated in that society. Sanskrit has ninety-six words for love; ancient Persian has eighty, Greek three, and English only one. This is indicative of the poverty of awareness or emphasis that we give to that tremendously important realm of feeling. Eskimos have thirty words for snow, because it is a life-and-death matter to them to have exact information about the element they live with so intimately. If we had a vocabulary of thirty words for love and matters of feeling, we would immediately be richer and more intelligent in this human element so close to our heart. An Eskimo probably would die of clumsiness if he had only one word for snow; we are close to dying of loneliness because we have only one word for love. Of all

6

the Western languages, English may be the most lacking when it comes to feeling. Imagine what richness would be expressed if one had a specific vocabulary for the love of one's father, another word for love of one's mother, yet another for one's camel (the Persians have this luxury), still another for one's lover, and another exclusively for the sunset! Our world would expand and gain clarity immeasurably if we had such tools.

It is always the inferior function, whether in an individual or a culture, that suffers this poverty. One's greatest treasures are won by the superior function but always at the cost of the inferior function. One's greatest triumphs are always accompanied by one's greatest weaknesses. Because thinking is our superior function in the English-speaking world (that is, the generally prevailing value or ideal, even if many individuals do not conform to this pattern), it follows automatically that feeling is our inferior function. These two faculties tend to exist at the expense of each other. If one is strong in feeling, one is likely to be inferior in thinking—and vice versa. Our superior function has given us our science and the highest standard of living the world has ever known—the envy of the third world—but at the cost of impoverishing the feeling function.

This is vividly demonstrated by our meager vocabulary of feeling words. If we had the expanded and exact vocabulary for feeling that we have for science and technology, we would be well on our way to warmth of relatedness and generosity of feeling.

It is instructive to examine a culture such as India's to see what patterns they have evolved. When one makes this journey halfway around the world one quickly sees that they have a wealth of vocabulary and corresponding consciousness in the realm of feeling but suffer a crushing poverty in awareness of the practical elements of science, politics, and planning. One can learn so much by observing a society that has exactly the opposite pattern of inferiority and superiority from our own. We are rich where they are poor; they are rich where we are poor. I was sobered to learn that the Japanese could not function in the complexity of World War II in their native tongue and were forced to use English for some of the activity that the feeling- and sensation-oriented Japanese language could not encompass. It is amusing to hear the Indian feeling-oriented languages proceeding with the addition of such terms as line voltage, fuse box, and coaxial cable. Our own language is being enhanced by such terms borrowed from the East as Mandala,

Yoga, and Zen. Each language is enriching its poverty-stricken neighbor.

A MYTHICAL APPRAISAL OF OUR
WOUNDED FEELING FUNCTION

Fortunately we have two myths in our heritage that surmount the language problem and go straight to the heart of the dilemma of feeling. These two are the myth of the Fisher King, which is a fragment of the Grail Myth, and the myth of the Handless Maiden. These two great cultural treasures, one from the twelfth century and the other from a slightly later period, tell us of the wounded feeling function. One is eloquent in its description of wounded masculinity and the other of wounded femininity.*

Men and women suffer quite differently from the wounding of their feeling functions, and much of the

---

*I am reasonably at home in discussing the masculine dimension of this ubiquitous problem, but I embark on the feminine dimension of it with some trepidation. I refer the reader to Gertrude Nelson's book *Here All Dwell Free* (Valentine, 1993) for her feminine wisdom on this dimension of the wound.

tension and lack of communication between man and woman springs from this difference. There are many parallels between the masculine and feminine woundings but some marked differences also. The two myths will illustrate this eloquently.

The twelfth century began so many of the issues that we struggle with today. It has been said that the winds of the twelfth century have become the whirlwinds of the twentieth century. Thus we can profitably look at the road maps of Western civilization laid down in the formative time of our modern world to gain some perspective on the maze that we encounter today. The story of the Fisher King is more pertinent today than one would ever guess at first hearing. Most men are wounded fisher kings now and it is important to see how we suffer these wounds and how they began. We are profoundly indebted to the bards, artists, and storytellers who cherished these insights through dark times and delivered them safely to us. We need them badly. Only myth or art can hold a matter as profound as feeling.

We are examining the wounding of both men and women, and though the Fisher King speaks directly to men, it is applicable to the masculine side of women.

In a similar way the Handless Maiden speaks to the feminine side of a man.

The story of the Fisher King is the chronicle of that part of us wounded in the great development in other spheres that occurred in the twelfth century. Science, individuality, a new sense of freedom, romanticism—all of these were taking on new power and definition at that time. If this had not happened, our culture would have remained medieval and we would still be in the primitive state that prevails in much of the third world to this day. It was a wonderful explosion of new human faculties, but cost a heavy price. The story of the Fisher King is the story of that wound that fell principally on the feeling function.

Part One

THE FISHER KING

LET US NOW HEAR THE story of the fisher king and how he bore the wounds of his time.

THE WOUNDING

There is a young prince in his teens who is out doing his knight errantry, as is the duty of every youth, when he stumbles onto a camp in the woods with no one about. A fire burns under the grate and a salmon lies roasting on the spit. The prince is young, hungry, and impulsive, and the salmon smells so good that he reaches out to take some of it to assuage his hunger. The salmon is very hot and burns his fingers, causing him to drop it. When he puts his fingers into his mouth to ease the burn, he gets a bit of the salmon into his mouth. This wounds him so badly that he lies in agony for all the rest of his life but for the last three days.

There are variations in the story: some say that he is wounded in the thigh by the taste of the salmon, others say that one of the owners of the camp comes back at this moment, sees the interloper eating the salmon, and shoots an arrow through his two testicles, an arrow that can neither be driven through nor pulled out. Yet another story tells of a wound by a poisoned sword in the thigh. All of the stories agree that the young prince is wounded in the generative region of his being.

The fisher king wound is in the male, generative, creative part of a man's being. It is a wound intimately connected with his feeling function and affects every sense of value in his psychological structure. This is the price we have paid for the cool, precise, rational, and scientific world that we have won at so high a cost. We are trained that objectivity, scientific thought, and dispassionate reasoning are possible only when feelings are discounted. We rarely differentiate feeling from emotion, and most people cannot tell the difference.

The fisher king's wound leaves him cold and he is never again able to be warm. It is eloquent that the slang expression for a sophisticated person is "cool." We may die of our "coolness," which is one of the characteristics of a fisher king–wounded man. One feels this coldness around people who are feeling wounded and they seem to reply to warmth or relatedness in some objective or dispassionate manner that stops all feeling "cold" in its tracks. It is as if such a person were unable to see over his own woundedness and contact another on a human level. Women are so often hurt by this wound in their men and often have little insight into what disturbs them so deeply. The fisher king's wounding in the thigh is symbolic of our difficulty in directly sexual matters. But it also represents wounding of other generative functions: one cannot create or produce at one's job, has dried up, or perhaps lacks warmth or attentiveness when tenderness would be appropriate.

I was about to erase the last sentence as being cold and calculating, when I am talking about a warm and vibrant subject; but I leave it as an example of the coldness that can creep into Western thought before one knows what has happened to him! It is blasphemy to talk about the appropriateness of tenderness; the

17

English language flows into such terrible forms so easily! Poetry or song would save us from this coldness but that is not proper in this context.

The German version of our story has an even more violent interpretation of the wounding of the fisher king. In Von Eschenbach's telling of the story, a terrible collision occurs between the nature of light and dark, which reverberates down to our own time with its tensions and violence.

The young prince—soon to be the fisher king—rides out one day with a banner reading *Amour* on his staff. Rightly so, for he is in search of Love and prepared to give his all for this youthful version of the splendor of God. But he is soon deflected from his vision of Love and union by the appearance of a pagan knight recently come from the Holy Land. This contradictory fact is the beginning of the fisher king's agony, for who can cope with the contradiction that the pagan element comes from the Holy Land? The young fisher prince reverts to his medieval heroic training: he lowers his javelin and rides at full tilt to kill the pagan knight.

What a tragic transformation has occurred! The youth who at one moment was the champion of Amour, the principle of Love, is in an instant transformed into an engine of destruction and ready to kill any male simply because these are the customs of chivalry and the heroic way. I know of no worse moment in mythology, and the issue is but another statement of those terrible-wonderful events in our psychological history such as the expulsion from the Garden of Eden or Prometheus's theft of fire.

In the German version the young prince is named Amfortas, meaning he who is without power. Almost always, he who is without power is the one who boasts and is led into reckless confrontations that are not necessary. It is possible that Amfortas is so named because he inherited his power without having won it by his own effort. Titled power, not yet legitimately won, is powerless.*

Power is never lost but can easily be deflected or misplaced. So the stage is set for high drama when Amfortas, the powerless one, faces the pagan knight, who has all the power of his natural and instinctive maleness.

The two clash and there is a dreadful wounding and destruction. The pagan knight is killed and Amfortas is castrated. A bit of the pagan knight's javelin remains embedded in Amfortas's thigh and the unbearable

---

*I am indebted to Joseph Campbell for this insight.

wound of the fisher king begins. He is described as being too ill to live but unable to die. No better description of our modern neurotic structure has ever been formulated.

The young prince—soon to be king—of the realm is now rendered impotent and the natural maleness of youth has been killed. The feeling function (under the banner of Amour) is left impotent and the natural man is dead. One recalls Gawain's statement at King Arthur's court that "everything has been won by the lance and everything has been lost by the sword." Discrimination—the lance—has brought maleness to its most creative level; brute force—the sword or javelin—has destroyed everything and left instinct dead and the young prince impotent.

Later in the story the tip of the javelin from the pagan knight is withdrawn from the unhealed wound of the fisher king and the word *Grail* is discovered engraved on it. Joseph Campbell describes this as spirit—the Grail—being carried by instinct—the pagan knight. It takes a man of high integrity to understand that the very highest attainment of his masculine nature is accomplished by the power of his instinct. Anything less would not have the power to see the evolution of the highest form of manhood to its apex. The loftiest forms of idealism and love have no power unless they operate with the blessings of instinct. Any idealism not grounded in instinct is doomed to failure.

On another level, our story is telling us that a dreadful mistake occurred when our culture took the view that spirit is to be attained by the suppression of nature and instinct. Spirit can attain its divine heights only with the power of nature to provide the strength for its fulfillment.

One can proceed with one's spiritual journey only with the understanding that opposites are constantly close to each other. It is never a matter of one vanquishing the other but a matter of each performing its proper function. Only too often the cultural man kills his natural man and nature replies by making the cultural man impotent. What more accurate statement of our modern dilemma can be made?

The young prince, soon to be king of the land, suffers so severely that he is unable to stand erect and incapable of performing his duty to the kingdom, which withers under his neglect. Only one thing assuages his suffering; he feels a little better when he is fishing. When he is occupied with fishing from his boat in the moat surrounding his castle, his suffering is diminished. Otherwise he lies on his litter in his castle suffering a terrible agony. This can be interpreted as saying that a wounded person finds life bearable only when he is engaged in some contact with the unconscious. Poetry, artistry, teaching, and healing are such activities that assuage the wound of the fisher king. They do not heal the dreadful wound but they make life bearable while one makes his way to the true healing.

The fisher king wound is to be seen on the face of almost any man who passes on the street; the ache of life, the anxiety, dread, loneliness, the corners of the mouth pointing down—all are summed up by the fisher king wound.[1]

EATING THE SALMON

What a curious wounding this is! Why should a bit of salmon produce so grievous a wound? And why should the wound be specifically in the thigh—the generative and creative part of a man?

Salmon is one of the many symbols for Christ. Christ is the fish that is the carrier of the splendor of God on the face of the earth. A bishop wears a miter, shaped like the head of a fish, to indicate that he is the successor to Christ. An early symbol of a Christian was the stylized fish made by the overlapping of two circles. In early days one could draw half of such a figure in the dust without disclosing one's meaning—a circle was innocent enough—unless another Christian was present. The other would recognize the symbol, draw the other half of the fish, and make contact with a fellow Christian.

A very old Coptic treatise contains an illustration of Christ in a boat fishing for a fish, which is himself. This is another way of describing the importance of the fish and its closeness to the unconscious in this process. Alchemical and Coptic stories love to make these circular statements that speak of the finding of one's self by one's self.

So the salmon is Christ, or the carrier of Christ, and getting a bit of salmon into one's mouth is equivalent to a First Communion that one is not yet ready to take. This is much like the innocence of the Garden of Eden being broken by the eating of the forbidden fruit. Like Adam, the young prince took something that did not belong to him, or in a more generous interpretation, took something before he could cope with it. And like Adam, he suffered a tremendous guilt and had to cover his thighs. Adam got off with a fig leaf and guilt; the fisher king had to carry an unhealed wound in the thigh. The fisher king is clearly a second Adam going through the advent of consciousness.

A Buddhist doctrine indicates that all suffering (that is, psychological suffering such as a fisher king wound) comes from an experience of the splendor of God that is too great to bear. In this manner of thinking, one can say that the fisher king wound resulted from the nature of Christ in the salmon, too great or too soon for the young prince to bear. Too much or too soon leads directly to suffering. One's first contact with God in a conscious way is quite certainly to be experienced as a wounding.

As Gawain tells King Arthur at the Round Table, "We have won everything by the lance and lost everything by the sword." This is to say that a high and noble value is to be won by discrimination, sacrifice, healing, and the work of consciousness; but everything will be lost by that brute force and power that the sword represents. The lance is a healer; the sword is a killer. It was the lance that pierced the side of Christ on the cross. To this day in the Eastern Orthodox churches, the host is fractured at the Mass by piercing it with a lance. Fine focus will win the kingdom; power and brute force will wreck it. If one can understand the redeeming lance nature of maleness and the brute sword destruction by maleness he has the differentiated tools necessary for the masculine journey.

There is a fashion today to let maleness express itself in its most violent and brutal aspects without regard to consequences. But a choice is possible between brutality—always destructive—and discrimination—the essence of the masculine faculty of intelligent choice.

It is the feeling function, the sense of valuing, that suffers the fisher king wound in most Western people. One hears the complaint from so many modern men that the outer circumstances of their lives are better than ever before, two cars in the garage, shorter work hours than ever before, vacations in far and exotic places—but life has lost its savor. No outer things—new car, better vacation, more money, or a new wife—can assuage this fisher king wound. It is a wounding of the very capacity for feeling and cannot be cured on any other level. No physical object or thinking can reduce the suffering and wounded feelings or restore the generative capacity of the fisher king.

I am often puzzled in going to India to see people who have so little in an outer sense but have so much happiness. Or I have only to drive thirty miles from my house, crossing the border into Mexico, to see people living below the poverty level, in our terms, being happier than the lucky Americanos north of the border. It is as if we have gained the highest technical civilization in the history of the world but at the cost of losing the simpler virtues of happiness and contentment. Aldous Huxley once commented that we have made the ceiling of yesterday's desire the floor of today's expectations.

I once asked a friend in India if we could talk about the problem of loneliness, the worst expression of the wounded feeling function. He replied that he had never been lonely in his life so he had nothing to say on the subject. This was a more eloquent reply than anything else he could have said. Here was an unwounded man who did not experience loneliness and anxiety as the constant companions that are so common in the West.

This can be understood only in terms of the fisher king wound—whatever language one uses for it. He who is badly wounded in the thigh—in his feeling function—will not be happy over anything; he who is less wounded, or like peasant people in the third world countries, unwounded by the guilt of self-consciousness, will have a measure of happiness that is the secret envy of all complicated societies. What educated person does not have fantasies about a South Seas island paradise or the nobility of peasant life? Generally the more intelligent the person and the more highly educated, the worse is the wound. The hippie movement of the sixties was a serious attempt to restore our unwoundedness and do away with fisher king wounds. It failed since one cannot go back to a simpler time but only forward to the healing of the fisher king wound, which is the goal of our story.

The term *fisher king* is appropriate since the young prince is so much associated with fish; first he is wounded by a fish (the unlawful taking of consciousness, which was called the fruit of the forbidden tree in the Adam and Eve story), then he is partly relieved of his suffering while fishing. To fish in this sense is to do one's inner work—work on dreams, meditation, active imagination, drawing, music, or poetry—any form of inner work that is rich to one. Even such mundane things as gardening and getting a "runner's high" are fishing in this sense since they put one in contact with the inner world. Fishing is a fisher king's only balm to his aching wound.

To translate this into more immediate terms, eating the salmon is taking on consciousness before one is mature enough to support it. What teenage boy has not blundered into someone's camp (psychologically speaking), taken on power or authority that he was not yet able to handle, and suffered a humiliating defeat that leaves him with the sword or arrow wound of the fisher king? What young man has not tried some adult task with bravado only to find that he could not accomplish it? The humiliation, embarrassment, and feelings of inferiority engendered by such a venture cause a fisher king wound in him and suffering that is particularly deep and painful. Perhaps it was a brash love affair or trying to climb the sheer face of a cliff or a business venture that he was not skillful enough to manage. A man tortures himself at 2:00AM with these memories.

It is tragic that many modern men never escape the fisher king wound and live in anxiety and inferiority all their lives.

THE MEANING OF WOUNDEDNESS

One wonders why it is necessary that a part of one be so badly wounded as our story portrays. But many legends inform us that we must pay a price for the departure from the Garden of Eden and the journey to

higher realms of consciousness. An Eskimo shaman's
tale gives a clue: The good spirits needed a new
shaman in an Eskimo community to replace the old
shaman who had died. They chose an adolescent boy
to be trained for this role. They took him into the un-
derworld and cut him up into pieces so that no two
bones touched each other. Then the evil spirits came
and gnawed all the flesh from the exposed bones.
When the future shaman was completely gnawed bare
and not one bone touched another, the good spirits re-
turned, put all the bones back together again (being
very careful not to lose any bone since the new shaman
would be without this part of his body if anything was
mislaid), put new flesh on his reconstructed bones, and
welcomed him into the tribe as the new shaman. A
record was kept of all the evil demons who had
gnawed on his bones, since the new shaman had the
power to cure illnesses caused by such demons. He
was unable to cure any illness caused by an evil demon
that was not present at his dismemberment.

This is to say that the fisher king wound is the
preparation for consciousness (our modern word for
shaman power) and the suffering is the training for
the future healer or genius. Anything not experienced
in the training-suffering is also missing in his later

power. When choosing a healer it is important to know what he has experienced and whether he has the power to heal the specific illness that his patient brings to him.

This is the background of any healer, inventor, seer, artist, teacher, or creator who has true power. Anyone who is arrested midway in the process is a tragic failure, a healer who did not experience the reintegration after his dismemberment. If one has been very badly wounded in the fisher king experience, this danger is great.

The Fisher King's Realm

To take our story in its innermost dimensions, the king is the ruler of one's inner domain and sets the character and tone of one's life. If the king (that is, the central focus of one's personality) is wounded, then the whole personality will be troubled and there will be no productiveness. Since it is the generative part of the fisher king that is wounded, it is the generative part of the personality that is impaired. The fisher king's land is described as unproductive—the cattle do not breed, the crops do not grow, the orchards do not bear, wives are widowed, and men are in despair. One finds himself uncreative in every realm. A modern man would complain that he has no new ideas, he is stale, bored, stuck, uncreative, and depressed. If the king is wounded the land is barren.

We have noted that it is our feeling function that gives a sense of joy, worth, and meaning to life. It may seem strange that the meaning of life should be in the hands of the feeling function rather than in one's reasoning capacity, but this is the case. No one ever succeeded in finding a reason for living by the reasoning process. Carl Jung spoke of the patient who believed that life was an incurable illness with a very bad prognosis. There is no rational argument against this! If it were possible to base one's life on reasoning we would only require intelligence to plumb the meaning of life. But it is the feeling function that gives meaning and worth. Life is precarious when its deepest meaning is in the hands of so unpredictable and undisciplined a faculty as our collectively inferior feeling.

What happens when the feeling function is wounded and turns dark? Our story tells us in mythical terms that we lie on a litter groaning in agony or have to spend our time fishing to gain some respite. By middle life much of our feeling life is wounded. Another perspective yields a

31

startling survey of wounded feelings. Anything that is put back into the unconscious (as when the fisher king drops the salmon that he has just picked up) once it has been in consciousness, turns dark and becomes a symptom in one's psychological structure. What has been a conscious part of one's philosophy or attitude one moment can become a symptom and have compulsive power over one the next moment if one drops or refuses it. It is understandable that the young fisher king should drop the salmon when it is too hot for him and he is too young to bear its splendor; but understandable or not, a new potential vision retreats to the realm of symptom as a result and the fisher king suffers almost unrelieved agony for many years.

Carl Jung comments on this from a historical perspective; he observes that when humankind dropped the Greek pantheon of gods (a conscious and rich statement of our interior structure), humankind immediately became the prey to a host of symptoms that characterize us now. We no longer have Zeus but have headaches instead. We no longer have Aphrodite and her noble feminine realm but we have gastric upsets. To dethrone anything from consciousness to unconsciousness is to diminish it in stature to a symptom. It follows directly from this that the cure of any psychological symptom requires that we make that content conscious again and restore it from compulsion to faculty. One should never undertake an inner development unless one is ready to see it through lest that development drop back into the unconscious and leave one worse than before. Senator Byrd, that venerable man from the South, replied to an argument in the Senate at the beginning of World War II that a little bit of (monetary) inflation would not hurt anything by saying, "There is no such thing as a little bit of inflation any more than there can be a little bit of pregnancy." One should not touch a new consciousness without taking it the whole way of its development.

Faculty (the new consciousness available to the fisher king in the form of the salmon) can only too easily slip back into the unconscious and instantly reappear as a symptom, the fisher king wound, so that the same energy is now experienced as suffering.

THE GRAIL CASTLE

Thus far our story has been a very sad one, the story of a superior man, the young prince who is the future king of the realm, being badly wounded and exiled to suffering. Mythology never leaves us stranded; no matter what a dark tale it may spin, a true myth will lead us out of the dilemma and offer a cure. The Grail myth does this in splendid terms and gives us one of the greatest visions of healing and wholeness of any mythology.

Carl Jung has stated that Christianity is the best existing road map of the Western soul; the Grail myth uses this profound language to describe the healing of the fisher king wound.

We find that the fisher king's castle is the keeper of the Holy Grail, the cup from which Christ gave the Last Supper. Every night in the fisher king's castle there is a wonderful procession: a fair damsel carries the Patton, the plate that supplied the bread at the Last Supper; another carries the lance that was used to pierce the side of Christ on the cross; still another carries the Grail itself, which glows with a light from within and brings the procession to a climax. Each person in the royal assemblage in the castle is served from the Grail and instantly receives what he wishes even though the wish is not articulated. Everyone, that is, except the fisher king, who lies on his litter groaning with his unhealed wound and without the solace of his daily fishing. He tries to receive the nourishment and healing of the Holy Grail, but because of his wound, he is unable to take the healing.

Probably the worst pain ever experienced is the self-inflicted suffering that has no cure outside one's self. To be near something beautiful or precious but to be unable to experience it is the subtlest possible form of torture. To live in affluence, have everything one ever dreamed of having, success and ownership beyond the kings of earlier times, but to find all of this ashes in one's mouth is the particular kind of existential suffering that is the lot of modern fisher kings. This is stated eloquently in the symbol of the fisher king being lord of the Grail castle and having the Grail immediately before him—but being unable to touch it. A fortune that one cannot enjoy, a marriage where there is an unbridgeable gulf between the partners, a fine body that no longer brings the runner's high that used to thrill one, the sound of applause that no longer affirms the performer—these are modern statements of the worst of all wounds, the fisher king wound.

At the worst of my own fisher king wound, I was driving to my parents' house for Christmas when I found a performance of Handel's Messiah advertised at Grace Cathedral in San Francisco that evening. I delayed my journey by half a day so I could partake of this favorite music performed in the best possible setting. Twenty minutes into the performance I found I was the wounded fisher king in the Grail castle and in the unendurable suffering of being in the presence of pure beauty but unable to partake of it. The fisher king wound stood like a barrier between me and the music, and I could not endure the closeness to something so valuable accompanied by the prohibition from touching it. I had to leave the cathedral and drive half the night in my isolation. The fisher king wound in me was so deep at that time that I was alienated from anything of beauty. No outer barrier stood between me and the beauty of the music; but my own sense of alienation made it impossible to partake of that beauty. No suffering is more unendurable than the presence of beauty that one cannot accept.

THE HEALING OF THE FISHER KING WOUND

A true myth always prescribes for the problem that it lays forth. Like any great work of art, it follows the pattern of darkness being redeemed by light. The darkness of our story thus far is the despair and isolation of the wounded fisher king, a suffering that has reached its apex in our own time. And the redemption of that darkness? Where is a cure to be found for so pervasive a problem?

The answer is to be found in a most unexpected place, in the blunderings of an innocent fool who has it in his power to release the agony of the suffering fisher king.

The legend of an innocent fool who will one day find his way into the Grail castle and bring the healing of the fisher king has long been known in the land so ravaged by the wounding of their king. In its simple language the myth promises that one day a young man, entirely innocent of his great mission, will wander into the Grail castle, see the magnificent procession that is enacted every night, and, if he asks the one pertinent question, will relieve the fisher king's suffering and remove the blight from the land.

What a power to have! And what an unexpected place for it to be lodged!

It is Parsifal—not by chance his name means Innocent Fool—who brings this healing power, and we now examine his story that has given him so much curative power.

It is humbling to find that the wounded fisher king is totally at the mercy of an innocent fool to bring the precious healing for his suffering. This is to say that the deepest part of ourselves, the king, can be healed only by a boyish, inventive, capricious, youthful quality.

PARSIFAL

Parsifal, our innocent fool, was born after his father's death. Redeeming heroes so often have difficult parenting and Parsifal obeys this pattern by growing up with no father and the loss of all of his brothers who had been killed before his birth. His mother, Heart's Sorrow, has lost her knight husband and all of her sons to the foolishness of chivalry and the customs of her time that all aristocratic males shall spend their time in knight errantry and heroic battles. Heart's Sorrow understandably decides to keep Parsifal's parentage secret from him and he grows up knowing nothing of the heritage of chivalry that flows in his veins. His mother keeps him in the garden of innocence and clothes him in a single garment of homespun that symbolizes his rustic upbringing. But one day Parsifal comes onto a party of five knights and his innocence is broken and he must follow the pattern of his ancestors and make his way into the heroic world.

Parsifal has many adventures and finds himself drawn into the court of King Arthur, where he is knighted. He finds an excellent teacher, Gournemont, who gives him all the equipment for the life of a true knight. But even Gournemont is unable to convince Parsifal to abandon the ridiculous homespun garment that his mother imposed upon him. This homespun single garment is to play a vital role in Parsifal's story when there is a collision between the garment and his fateful duty to ask the redeeming question at the Grail castle. One can best understand this symbolism by seeing the homespun as Parsifal's mother complex—that inborn tendency in every man to look backward and be caught in an infantile wish for the security of mother and infancy. To be clothed in this regressive tendency is the worst impediment to the redeeming power of masculinity. It is a poignant moment when Parsifal defends his mother's homespun against all the teaching and examples of his guide and compatriots.

Parsifal has attained enough manhood to be on his knight errantry and we find him riding on his horse through a forest one evening just before dusk. There is no place to stay the night and he faces the lonely and cold prospect of sleeping in the woods without shelter.

But just as he is resigned to this prospect, he comes upon a lake with a lone fisherman in a small boat. He hails the fisherman—who is none other than the fisher king spending his time in the one thing that brings him any relief from his suffering—and asks if there is any place to stay the night. The fisherman replies that there is no dwelling within thirty miles. Then, in contradiction to this statement, the fisherman continues by inviting Parsifal to his own house. "Just down the road a little way, turn left, cross the drawbridge, and you will be my guest for the night." This simple set of instructions is so powerful that one should memorize it deeply within his consciousness since it will be the formula for finding the way out of the fisher king wound when one is in the grip of its suffering. And one may take note that it is the suffering fisher king within one that offers the first directive for his own cure.

First, the fisher king says there is no dwelling within thirty miles, a way of saying mythologically that there is nothing in the three-dimensional world which will help one in any practical way. But then he goes on to say that by following specific instructions a place of comfort and safety is not far away. The specific instructions are to go down the road—whatever road one is involved with at the moment—turn left, which is to say go toward the unconscious or the world of imagination and fantasy, cross the drawbridge—the division between our conscious world and the inner world of imagination—and one will be in the Grail castle, the miraculous place of healing.

What a promise contained in so simple a set of instructions! As was promised in the old myth known to the people in the Grail castle, here is the formula for the redemption of their suffering king. It is equally effective for the suffering king that resides in the breast of nearly every modern man.

Parsifal follows the instructions, goes down the road a little way, turns left, and crosses the drawbridge, which snaps closed the moment he has crossed it, ticking the back hooves of his horse. This nearly unseats him but he survives this test of balance and strength. Many a youth gets as far as the drawbridge of his healing only to be thrown from his horse by this test.

Parsifal is welcomed into the Grail castle, brought to the awesome procession that goes on every night and watches mutely as the miracle of the Grail brings its healing to everyone present—except the fisher king, who is unable to partake of the miracle.

Since every detail of a myth is important and no event, no matter how insignificant, is without meaning, we are instructed that the healing vision of our lives occurs every night in our interior Grail castle. It is in the hidden world of dreams and imagination that the miracle is presented every night. The healing is never far away—either in distance or time; only down the road a little way and turn left to find that the great drama of healing takes place every night of our lives!

But one detail isolates us from the healing of the fisher king at this point in the story. Everything has been accomplished for the prophesied healing of the fisher king—all but one detail. Parsifal does not ask the prescribed question, Whom does the Grail serve? That is, Parsifal does not make the experience conscious. Because of this failure the great procession in the Grail castle comes to a close as in countless nights before and the fisher king remains unable to drink from the healing Grail and remains suffering on his litter.

What a terrible drama! Is it true that every youth comes this close to the redemption of his suffering and fails the one essential question which would end the alienation of his life? Yes; this is the psychological history of virtually every modern man. He is offered a vision of the meaning of his life in his mid-teens but cannot find the strength of consciousness to accept it. The first meeting fails, inevitably. Who can stand the first—or the hundredth—vision of beauty that he has seen? But later a mature meeting after one has done his work in the world brings the consciousness—the question—that is healing.

Why? What is this mute prohibition which keeps Parsifal from asking the question which would give him citizenship in the Grail castle and healing to the suffering fisher king? Parsifal takes the gifts of consciousness but fails to reply with his own act of consciousness.

Though I can find no mention of this in any of the myths, I think it is Parsifal's inability to put off his mother's single homespun garment (his mother complex) which alienates him and makes him inarticulate at the critical moment. Perhaps redemption cannot come so early and the great drama of one's life would not be complete if Parsifal consciously experienced so great a vision early in his life.

Parsifal spends the night in the Grail castle, awakens in the morning to find no one about, saddles his horse, crosses the drawbridge, and is back in the ordinary world of time and space.

The myth tells us that he then spends the next twenty years in the exhausting work of rescuing fair maidens, fighting dragons, relieving besieged castles, and aiding the poor—all the male experiences which intervene between early youth and middle age when one has a second chance to visit the Grail castle. Fate is kind and allows us two chances in life when the veil between consciousness and the unconscious grows thin. One of these is mid-adolescence when one is gratuitously allowed to see a great vision and the other is in mid-life when he has a second chance to touch his visionary life if he has earned the right. The Grail castle is close at hand every night of one's life and may be experienced at any time; but it is most easily accomplished at these two critical times of one's life.

The middle portion of a man's life is then recounted in Parsifal's story; all the maidens and dragons and noble deeds which fill the middle section of a man's life are recounted and we find him again at a time when he is capable of touching the Grail castle.

The Parsifal we find this time is a middle-aged man, weary, worn, and tired of the heroic journey. Fair maidens have lost their charm and dragons no longer inspire him to heroic action. Parsifal has worn out the youthful activity of his life and it has gone dry. But he has put off his mother's homespun garment in all this activity and is now free to bring his unimpaired maleness to the Grail castle.

One day Parsifal is trudging along on his horse when a group of pilgrims challenge him: "Why are you in full armor on the day of the death of our Lord? Don't you know it is Good Friday?" No, Parsifal does not know it is Good Friday and has little interest in such things. But the pilgrims convince him to take off his armor and go for confession with them to a hermit who lives nearby. The old hermit is severe with Parsifal and recounts all of his sins and mistakes to him. The worst of these mistakes is that he failed to ask the burning question at the Grail castle, which would have redeemed the suffering fisher king. Parsifal understands the great vista of his life and is recalled instantly to the principal duty of his life, to heal the suffering fisher king. The old hermit instructs Parsifal, "Go down the road a little way, turn left, cross the draw-bridge. . . ." Here is the same instruction from twenty years earlier! True: the Grail castle is never more than a little distance down the road, then turn left; but it is only when a man is at his best—by naivete in his youth or by having earned the right in his middle age—that he is capable of seeing that sublime fact. The Catholic Church presents this in its medieval formulation when it says that the Grace of God is always available but man must ask for it before it is effective.

Parsifal regains the Grail castle easily and finds himself in the great hall with the divine procession before him. This time he asks the crucial question, Whom does the Grail serve? and is instantly made aware of its answer, The Grail serves the Grail King. Only now we are informed that an old king lives in the Grail castle who never shows himself but who is the center of the castle and its great power. Parsifal is informed of the greatest secret of a man's life by this simple question and its equally simple answer. One discovers that the Grail King—a thinly disguised description of God—is as near as the Grail castle has been.

The meaning of life is not in the quest for one's own power or advancement but lies in the service of that which is greater than one's self. Carl Jung made this statement in more modern terms when he said that the meaning of life is to relocate the center of gravity of the personality from the ego to the Self. If asked what is the meaning of life, most people would answer that it is to serve me—my ego plans and involvements. The revelation of the Grail castle is that life serves something greater than one's self.

This requires a Copernican revolution to relocate the center of the universe from the ego to the Self. And that revolution is as painful in our personality as the Copernican revolution was in history.

A detail of the story is encouraging: Parsifal need only ask the question; he is not required to answer it. Once the question is asked the answer comes from a source greater than his store of personal wisdom.

The moment Parsifal asks the fateful question (that is, consents to consciousness) the wounded fisher king rises from his litter of suffering and is miraculously restored to health and strength. The whole kingdom rejoices at the return of their strong king and a great springtime of joy and life begins.

The healed fisher king dies after three days. This is a strange ending to his part of the story but it can be understood that the wounded part of ourselves can be left behind when it has served its function in the development of the mature man. Parsifal is the matured hero and the suffering of the fisher king is no longer required.

Our story has presented the healing of the wounded feeling function in mythological language, and the actual transformation in one's life is likely to be less dramatic and not just one glorious moment; still, the formula holds true.

THE RESTORED FEELING FUNCTION

One may inquire why all of this is associated with the feeling function. It is specifically so in our culture though in another set of circumstances it might be another faculty which is wounded, suffers for the traditional twenty years, and is restored by a heroic action of an intelligent man. Since it is the feeling function which is so neglected and wounded in our culture, this drama falls on that faculty in our experience.

We may be grateful for the mythology of the twelfth century, when so much of our modern world was beginning, for its definition of this wounding and its final healing.

Note

1. Much can be learned from a comparison of our Western heroic ideal with the East Indian view of the same material. Our Western ideal, which I grew up with and was not aware of any alternative to until I visited the East, is to make a heroic journey through life. That is best portrayed by the medieval knight, done up in his armor, helmet, and visor, sword in hand, javelin at the ready, waiting for anyone who will challenge him in the duel of chivalry. It was the heroic duty of a knight to find evildoers and run them through with his sword of righteousness. Dragons were specially the foe of knights, and the medieval stories tell countless tales of the great knight fighting some dragon that was holding the castle of a fair maiden under its tyranny.

Tournaments were the great delight of the medieval knight and he spent much of his time at this stylized form of fighting. If the knight later went out on a solitary quest for a fair maiden or the holy Grail and he came across another knight, visor was lowered, javelin was leveled, and the two knights went at each other in mortal combat. Each presumed he was fighting on the side of absolute right and his life was not too high a price to pay for this noble combat. In short, almost the whole content of life was devoted to right fighting wrong.

The East found a very different attitude toward the collisions of life. Their ideal was to search out the cause of the antagonism and reduce the tension between the warring opposites. They began with the basic assumption that nothing had a charge of energy unless it was in polarity to its opposite. It followed—gently—from that premise that if one could reduce either of the warring polarities, the other would diminish instantly and to the same degree. Conflict and hostility could thus be reduced by either or both parties concerned if one would reduce the vehemence of his own point of view.

Our heroic stance as seen through the eyes of an Eastern philosopher would seem to be the very formula for increasing hostility and producing an ever-escalating antagonism.

The young prince—soon to be the fisher king—follows the heroic ideal in our story and is immediately embroiled in a battle which can be nothing but destructive to both parties. This is the tragedy and near insolvable depth of our wounded feeling function that is so painful a burden to the Western world.

The legend of St. George and the dragon makes an interesting comment on the heroic ideal. English crusaders found the myth of St. George in the Middle Ages on one of their crusades, altered it to their own liking, and took it home as the epitome of English valor. The original form of the myth is as follows: St. George meets a dragon and goes into mortal combat with it. In a short time all three combatants, George, his horse, and the dragon, are mortally wounded. All three lie bleeding out their life on the ground. By chance, St. George has fallen under an orange tree (some say a lime tree) and by chance a bird pecks a hole in an orange directly over his mouth. A drop of the orange juice falls into St. George's mouth and revives him. He rises up with new strength, plucks an orange, squeezes the juice into his horse's mouth, and both rise up healed and strong. No one puts any juice into the dragon's mouth. The orange has long been a symbol of consciousness because of its similarity in shape and color to the sun.

This view of the disposition of energy in antagonism represents a more mature and realistic attitude than our traditional medieval triumph of good over evil.

Part Two

THE HANDLESS
MAIDEN

THUS FAR WE HAVE EXAMINED the wounded feeling function from a man's point of view. To explore woman's experience in this realm is to find many exact parallels and some startling differences. A man suffers his wound mainly in his generative faculty—be this directly in his sexual activity or indirectly in his inability to create in more subtle ways. A woman suffers an equal incapacity, in her generative or creative faculty, when her feeling function is wounded. But this wound appears in a woman in her inability to *do*, and it is no surprise to find in our myth of the woman's wounding that it is her hands that are damaged. In a wounded

woman her great cry is "What can I *do?* I feel so useless
or second-rate and inferior in this world that puts its
women on the rubbish heap when they are through with
courtship and childbearing!" Often this is accompanied
by a bitter hostility toward men who, in their male
chauvinistic attitude, keep her from any but second-rate
activities. In its thousand variations, woman's cry is
"What can I *do?*"

There are few good women's stories to give us insight into that feminine realm; it seems that most of
the stories have been told by men or about men and a
curtain is drawn over feminine mysteries. This is but
another example of the dominance of patriarchal values in our recent history. But fortunately, there are
three or four very good women's stories; we can take
one to guide us in this inquiry.

The myth of the handless maiden is the most eloquent portrayal of the wounding of the feeling function
as experienced by woman that is available to us. It is as
if it were addressed precisely to modern women, and
like all good myths, it states the problem and prescribes
its solution. As with the Grail myth, this story came
from a time in European history when our present attitudes were being formulated in those deep places where
the collective unconscious is generating the next step in

its evolution. Many versions of it appeared in Europe, showing the universality of the experience. We may be very grateful for the insights from this story.

Though much of the story revolves around men, it is not only men but also *masculinity* that is being described as the villain. Certainly, we have a long history of the subjection of women under the domination of men. But the problem is equally difficult in the tyranny that the masculine side of a woman exerts over her often helpless femininity. Marion Woodman once said in one of our joint lectures that the animus in a woman (the masculine component of a woman's psychology) can be as great a tyrant as any man!

THE DEVIL'S BARGAIN

The story of the handless maiden begins with a miller who has been grinding the grain for the village for as long as anyone can remember. He works hard, turning the millstone by hand and transforming natural grain into a civilized product, flour. This is honest work and the miller makes his contribution to the life of the village by his natural strength or occasionally with the aid of an animal who turns the millstone. This is a laborious process, limited by the strength of the miller or his animal. It has been so for as long as anyone can remember. "Ye shall earn thy bread by the sweat of thy brow" is the biblical law at this level of culture.

One day the devil appears and says, "For a fee [every satanic offer begins in this way] I will show you how to grind your grain with much less effort and much faster." The miller is immediately intrigued and makes a bargain with the devil. Certainly anything that takes less work and gives a greater output is beyond reproach. But the fee? That which stands in back of the mill. The miller presumes the devil means the old tree that stands behind the mill, something quite worthless and a very small price to pay for so handsome an improvement in his life.

So the devil brings his mechanical expertise and connects the millstone to a waterwheel so that the force of the stream running by the mill turns the stone effortlessly. The mill is now operating with its enhanced capacity, and truly it turns without effort and produces many times more flour than ever before. The miller is delighted; the miller's wife is busy with the extra income from the mill, and the miller is exploring what to do with his free time. Easier, faster, more is the great seduction for a modern mind. The miller's daughter is not concerned with this and continues her innocent life.

The miller is so pleased with his newly expanded life that he conveniently forgets that there is a price to pay and is surprised when the devil appears again some time later to demand his fee. The miller goes with the devil to get the old tree in back of the mill but is horrified to find that his daughter is standing there and the devil claims her as his price. The miller is desolate but unwilling to give up his much expanded mill, so he gives his daughter to the devil. The devil chops off her hands and carries them away. Another version of the tale has it that the devil claims the hands of the miller's wife as payment, but the old woman, too crafty to make any such bargain, agrees that the daughter shall lose her hands. In all the variations of the story, the daughter does not object.

A most terrible thing has happened! A mechanical advance has been won at the expense of the young feminine. This bargain is made many times a day by modern people. We buy a practical advance at the cost of a feeling value every time we give up our trip to the gym, or some weekend camping, or agree to more commuting on the freeway, in exchange for some practical goal. This is the miller's bargain, and it is legion. It is so deeply ingrained in our mentality that we fail to see it as a devil's bargain in its modern form. Like the miller who forgets that a price must be paid for his mill's increased efficiency, we think we can get practical advances at no cost. This delusion is so common in our modern mentality that grocery shops are full of its language: two for the price of one, or a second one for only one cent, or one third more for the same price, or this is marked down from $7.99 to $4.99. We don't feel satisfied unless we have gotten something for nothing in our everyday exchanges. The outer dimensions of this in the marketplace are not dangerous, but it is a very short step to the inner world of feeling and value. Outer logic so easily silences inner feelings. Many times a day one gives up some feeling value in exchange for an outer advantage.

The miller is the first mechanic in the modern world; he is the first one to make the stream do his work for him, and he pays a catastrophic price in the form of his daughter's hands. We are from a long line of millers, and the infection is deep. Many times a day in a modern life the young feminine pays the price, a further amputation, when one makes a devil's bargain and believes one can get something for nothing. We might reverse the proverb and say that when one gets something for nothing, he is very likely to get nothing for something in the feeling world. This "nothing" is the source of much of the emptiness that is so characteristic of our age.

All things in the world are free gifts of nature—air, sunshine, food, joy—and can be enjoyed without guilt or wounding. It is a trick of the devil to turn this natural bounty into a commodity in a money-dominated marketplace. This mechanization (psychologically speaking) wounds us to the core and ends in so much wreckage in the feeling function. Only a confusion of levels could wreak so much havoc.

This dilemma can be described as the contrast between the mother complex and the mother archetype. The mother complex is that regressive part of our psychology that wants to go back to an earlier level of adaptation and be cared for by a mother who gives all and requires no effort from one. The mother complex is the art of getting something for nothing by a regression of consciousness. The mother archetype is the bounty of nature, which gives us our life and all that we need for that life and which is anyone's legacy by the fact of being alive. The mother archetype is the art of living peaceably with the bounty of nature, which is pure gift and lies within the ecology of the natural order.

Which one of these—mother complex, which is pure poison, or mother archetype, which is pure gold—will rule our lives is entirely a matter of attitude. If one goes at life to see how much one can get out of it with the least effort or cost, then one is in the grips of the mother complex. If one is aware of the beauty and magnificence of life, one is experiencing the mother archetype. The issues at stake in this differentiation are the specific feminine values of regression or valuing.

Women are much wiser than men in this regard; few women make so clumsy and devastating a choice as the miller. But our masculine-dominated society has made many such choices and we have a huge legacy of mechanical advantages that are being paid for by a loss of feeling. To bring a bargain home from the marketplace is not wrong. I love a good bargain. But to gain a bargain at the expense of some inner value is extremely dangerous. To gain affection from another person without providing one's own part of the relationship is a devil's bargain. If one wants relatedness but will not give relatedness, this is the devil's bargain at its worst. To buy material comfort at the cost of feeling values is the devil's bargain.

If there is to be a highly trained surgeon on duty at the emergency hospital to care for my sudden appendicitis, someone must spend endless hours in school and internship to gain this skill. Someone must give up a part of his or her youth and spontaneity so that my physical world may be safeguarded. This is a fair bargain but a very sober one. The demand for luxury that indirectly costs one most of one's leisure is not so easily reconciled. The demand for sexual experience outside the framework of relatedness, whether by a man or a woman, carries a terrible cost paid by everything feminine. The devil's bargain comes in so many forms!

And who pays the bill for this bargain? Generally it is not the mature feminine, the miller's wife—for she is too hard-boiled, too canny to accept such a price, but the young feminine, the tenderest of one's feelings. It is the feeling life of which one is unaware that usually pays the price. Moods, depression, a general sense of malaise—these are the young feminine in one. Accepting the devil's bargain is one of the most despicable wrongs ever committed in the psychological world. To know the devil's bargains that are offered to us many, many times a day in the modern world is to begin to safeguard the young daughter, the tender feminine.

One faces the devil's bargain frequently when planning the structure of one's day. How much can one crowd into the day? How much can I get with minimum payment? How many times in the day does feeling (the daughter's hands) take second place to practicality?

How many days go by without music or the gym or a sunset walk? How many vacations are half-spoiled because the energy has been spent in a dozen devil's bargains before one even gets there?

This drama can be found on many different levels. Often the price of such a bargain is etched on the face of a man's wife, or much more frequently, on the self-confidence of his daughter. Or it may reside in the deepest part of the miller's feeling life, the center of his sense of worth and meaning.

Scapegoating is a favorite nonsolution to the problem of the devil's bargain. This ignoble art consists of putting one's own blame on another or some other situation and then banishing that other to oblivion (justifiable in one's own mind). Every small community, such as an office staff, a church, or a club, exists partly by the mechanism of scapegoating. A group of people will unconsciously choose an unfortunate individual and heap the community guilt upon him or her. Make the experiment of examining some small group of people you are involved with and observe the group maintaining its self-respect by looking down on some individual of that group. Every neighborhood has its scapegoat, every office its outcast, every church its pariah, every family its black sheep. In the larger world, one finds scapegoating in terms of races, nationalities, and color.

An alcoholic makes one of the worst devil's bargains; he trades his suffering for an oblivion paid by his wife, or more often, his daughter, in her oblivion as a personality. The nothingness that a woman often feels is frequently the nothingness that is the cost of a miller character near her. The daughter of an alcoholic is generally a handless maiden. She is frightened and incompetent, can't cope with life, and has an overwhelming sense of inferiority. Her first words in the face of a new challenge are "I can't." All this is the direct result of being "handless" as our story defines it. This may have been done to her without her permission if it occurred early in her life; or it may have been done with her permission if the strength of a family decision was in back of it. It is one of the terrible indictments of humankind that both the miller and his wife agreed to the scapegoating of the daughter. It is a terrible choice when one is faced with the alternatives of being handless or familyless.

A conspicuous example of this may be found in the recent history of Ethiopia. The old League of Nations looked the other way when Haile Selassie pointed out the rape of his country. The rest of the world—as great father and mother—agreed by default to this devil's bargain.

A man who fails to carry the father role for his children, even if he has been a brilliant success in life, will send his daughters into the world as handless maidens.

The inner level of this drama is much more subtle and difficult to trace. That is the wounding of the innermost feeling structure of the man himself. This manifests as bad moods, a feeling of worthlessness and incompetence, and an erosion of the values and meaning of life. To bargain away the young feminine is to lose the most precious dimension of a man's life and his sense of meaning in the world. This is a sober matter and closer to home than one realizes until he begins to explore his own handless maiden within. Wounded feelings, hurt, loneliness, worthlessness—these are the handless maiden within a man. No outer heroic action can restore meaning to a man's life if his tender feminine feeling value is damaged.

THE TRICKERY OF THE MACHINE

The Greek word *mechane,* which is the origin of our term *machine* as well as the root of *machination,* has a very sober connotation. Its root means to trick, and everything concerned with it has a dark character.

Dreams of mechanical things failing in their purpose often alert the dreamer that he or she is using devices or attitudes that are unworthy of his or her best nature. It is commonplace in the dreams of people who are capable of high consciousness that mechanical things do not work well. In their dreams an airplane journey is not completed, or the car does not deliver them to their destination. I remember the nightly dream of a young man in which a large commercial jetliner took off with a roar of power and a full complement of passengers— only to crash just past the end of the runway. This dream occurred most nights of his life for months. Because he was a superior person we can interpret this repeated dream to mean that he could not get by with a mechanical or contrived attitude toward life. His efforts at contriving a selfish way of life, which were basically trickery (mechanical in the sense of the word we are using here), were not working. His superior nature would not allow a cheap adaptation to life, no matter how sophisticated or ingenious it might be. When he understood this principle and gave up his egocentric attitude toward life, the dreams no longer needed to confront him with a plane crash every night.

I once dreamed that I had found the road to the Heavenly Jerusalem. I jumped into my little 1936 Ford (the first car I had ever owned, always a very special car in one's life). When I got to the top of the long winding road, the gatekeeper at the Heavenly Jerusalem told me that no cars were allowed there and I was to drive back down again and walk up the hill. Then I could have admittance to the Paradise Garden. I drove back down the hill, abandoned the car, and walked up the hill. Then I was allowed into the Heavenly Jerusalem. I have been working to divest myself ever since of the interior trickery represented by the car in my dream. Such trickery is the worst possible insulation against enlightenment or the Heavenly Jerusalem. I call it my 1936 Ford mentality.

A succession of philosophers have advised us to give up most of our mechanical aids so that our spiritual life might be the more vivid. Thoreau at Walden Pond, Mahatma Gandhi with his spinning wheel, Rousseau with his idealizing of primitive man, the hippie world trying to restore a simple way of life—these are all attempts to avoid inner trickery by diminishing the mechanical dimensions of the outer life. It's true that our overly complex outer way of life needs reappraisal, but it is the inner form of trickery that is the most deadly. We could abandon all our cars and computers and airplanes as advocates of simplicity advise but still keep the inner trickery that is the real source of the infamous devil's bargain. It is not necessary to give up outer things to avoid the devil; but it is necessary to abandon our nefarious struggle to get something for nothing.

All trickery exacts a heavy penalty. When the miller engages the devil's trickery, he also unwittingly agrees to the devil's price. Whenever you trick, psychologically speaking, you amputate the hands of your most tender feeling function, a price far too great for any outer advantage.

There is nothing wrong with the material dimensions of our mechanical devices, which are the envy of the rest of the world. I have heard it said that in an average household our labor-saving devices are the equivalent of twenty-seven servants as employed a century ago just to do the rudimentary chores. Owning a car, a computer, an airplane, and the host of other things we have around us as aids to our life are not wrong; but a mechanical view of life is wrong and extracts the feeling price. If an excess of "things" in life is eroding away one's peace, it is the attitude that is wrong, not the things. Trickery as attitude always involves getting something and refusing to pay the human, direct price for it. Mills are fine, increased production is excellent, new power is wonderful; but if they are obtained without direct conscious involvement with the process, they carry a price that will be unbearable at a later time.

Officials in New York City discovered that most of the schoolchildren in some ghetto districts, almost totally surrounded by their concrete world, did not know where milk came from. With the aid of some alert dairy officials, they constructed a tiny portable dairy with one cow, which went to each school and demonstrated feeding the cow, the milking process, bottling, and so forth. Milk meant more to those children after that and was not just something they got out of the refrigerator at the market. This is a naively simple example, but it illustrates how our culture is endangered on many levels by the mechanization of our living. Recently I drove through Amish country in the Midwest and saw the Amish farms—immediately distinguished by the fact that no electric power or telephone poles lead to the house—and encountered the little black horse-drawn buggies that are their only means of transportation. No motor, tractor, electric light bulb, pump, or telephone is ever used by an Amish family. This is a strict observation of an inner fact, but played out on an outer level. If people would observe their mechanical tendencies (trickery) on an inner level as carefully as the Amish observe their simple way of life outwardly, much suffering in the feeling world would be avoided. I was pleased at the sight of the Amish ways, but my intuition was that they are no less subject to inner trickery than we are. It would be a small price to pay for relief of our modern feeling woundedness if one had only to take down the power poles and adopt a little black buggy for transportation; but I think that has little to do with the issue. That would be attacking a virulent problem outwardly when it is inner in nature. A right solution on the wrong level is totally ineffective.

In Muslim countries, the old part of their cities is called the *medina,* or holy place. In this section of the city no car, motor, or engine-driven machinery is allowed, as it would disturb the spirituality of the center of the city. When I stood in the center of the *medina* of Fez in Morocco I watched with great care to see if there was tranquility on the faces of the people who lived there. Predictably, I saw that they had tried to make an outer solution to an inner problem and their lives were no more peaceful than in the modern cities. Like the Amish, they had addressed an inner problem in an outer way. It is our task to search out the mechanization of life in its inner dimensions, which is where the damage is done. A Hindu story speaks of this issue:

71

A holy man sat each morning under a banyan tree teaching the lesson of detachment from the Gita to his small audience of disciples. Among them was the king of the realm, taking his place like everyone else sitting on the ground before the great teacher. Also there was a sunyasin (a holy mendicant living in poverty) who owned nothing but his spare loincloth, which was hanging on the wall to dry, and a half skull, which was his begging bowl.

One day the sunyasin grew irritable and complained to the great teacher that it was unfair that the holy man treated the king, who lived in luxury, with as much deference as he did the sunyasin, who had given up everything but his spare loincloth, which was hanging on the wall to dry. The great teacher said nothing. (It is the custom of such teachers to reply indirectly to a question by some event of life a few hours or days later.)

Next day the little group was sitting at the feet of the great teacher when a messenger came to whisper some urgent news in the king's ear. The king did not move or take his attention from the teacher. Soon another messenger came with even more urgent news. When the third messenger

came it was plain for all to see that the news was
of a great fire that was sweeping down on the
royal palace across the river on the hill. Still another messenger came and shouted his information that the royal palace was in imminent danger
from the fire. All could now see the flames as they
came to the palace; in an incredibly short time, the
palace was entirely consumed by flames.

The great teacher continued his discourse on the
Gita and the king did not waver in his attention.

Soon the smell of smoke was carried to the little
group, then the crackling of the fire, then the adjoining trees were on fire.

When the little group could feel the heat of the
approaching fire, the sunyasin exploded in anxiety
and dashed to the wall to get his extra loincloth,
which was hanging there to dry. An instant later,
the smoke cleared and there was the palace in all
its serene splendor on the adjoining hill, with no
fire to be seen. The sunyasin came back to the little band of disciples with mute questioning on his
face. "And now who was attached to his property?" asked the holy man.

The great teacher had prepared a vivid example
for the sunyasin that physical possessions have

little to do with detachment. The king, with all his possessions, was engaging in less trickery than the sunyasir, who made such a show of asceticism. Attitude is much more important in the inner world than any outer mechanical or material alteration.

A king may be detached from his possessions and an ascetic owning nothing may be in the grips of his mechanical world. It is the attitude that is crucial, not the amount of property or mechanical things one has.

We are not talking about the physical things of our life but of the mechanical attitudes that we hold and the trickery they elicit from us. Mechanical aids are legitimate outwardly—there could be no culture without such things—but to grasp at something psychologically without paying its price is the inner trickery that costs such a heavy price. This is the devil's bargain.

Paying the Devil's Price

The miller (masculine) gets the benefit of the agreement with the devil while the young daughter (feminine) pays the price. It is obvious that no advancement in civilization can be made without some such bargain; to argue that civilization would be better served by staying with the hand-powered mill is to fall into the error of Mahatma Gandhi and Thoreau. But if we make a bargain, we must be wide awake to its terms. An advance in mechanical efficiency always costs a feeling price. The least we can do is be aware of this and pay the price as intelligently as possible. To pay this price intelligently is to be conscious of what we have done and the bargain we have made. Especially it means to be responsible for our own bargain and not scapegoat the price to someone else or unconsciously to our own inner feminine world of value, moods, and sense of worth. A conscious bargain retains its dignity and validity; an unconscious bargain creates a host of symptoms and meaningless suffering. The present manner of paying the price is most unintelligent and constitutes a large part of women's feeling that men have somehow betrayed them. The mill runs faster, but the daughter is left handless.

On closer examination this bargain is as painful to a man as to a woman, for it is often his inner, tender feeling qualities that pay the price. It is more difficult for a man to be aware of his inner nature because it is the young feminine—the most tender and sensitive parts of his inner nature—that is wounded. Virtually all of a man's feelings, sense of worth, sense of value, and moods are feminine. To wound the interior feminine in a man is to wound his whole feeling life and sense of worth. Since the feminine part of a man is usually less well developed than his masculinity, this sensitive part of his nature is often ignored and neglected. Most men are not even aware that it is their feminine side that is the keeper of all that is tender and precious in their lives! This means the naive, sensitive, largely unknown part of a man bears the cost. It is the usual lot of a man paying the devil's price to feel unhappy, tense, or anxious without knowing what has happened to him. This is the young feminine in its inarticulate woundedness, the miller's daughter.

Whether the drama goes on within a woman or is played out in the interior feminine part of a man, the story is much the same. If it is a woman's drama, her feminine values will be betrayed by an actual man (perhaps her father), the patriarchal culture around her, or her own masculine qualities dominating from within. If a man suffers this deadening trade, he may be dominated by some outer masculine tyrant or a private drama going on in his own psychology.

One can sympathize with Nehru*, who was caught between the archaic teaching of his mentor, Mahatma Gandhi, who advocated keeping India a rural and simple society, and the needs of the second-largest nation in the world trying to come out of its medieval character. The bargain that India struck is not working well; collective attempts are not the best approach to solving this difficult issue. I am more optimistic about what is possible for an intelligent individual, who can bring a sharper consciousness to bear than is found in any ponderous collective movement. When Dr. Jung was asked the question "Will we make it?" he always replied, "If enough individuals will do their inner work." There seem to be no collective solutions to this problem of wounded feelings, only individuals brave enough to take the problem personally. This is the new heroism.

ENTERING THE FOREST

Fortunately, myths not only diagnose but also prescribe. A real myth always provides a healing or cure for the ill that it describes. The healing for the handless

---

*The first prime minister of India after its independence in 1947.

maiden is a very curious one and not easily understood by our extroverted modern mentality.

For some time the handless maiden is content with her situation and does not complain. After all, there is enough money now to have servants in the household, and she does not have to do anything that would require hands. The unconscious of a family often takes very good care of its wounded members—mostly out of a sense of guilt at knowing, unconsciously, the origin of the wound. When the daughter complains that she cannot do anything, the mother replies that she does not have to. The daughter agrees to this explanation for some time. The feeling function, especially the young, naive form of it, is particularly vulnerable to arguments like this. "Well, what do I need hands for if everything is already taken care of?"

The family life goes on but the daughter grows more and more unhappy, withdrawn, and distressed. Her mechanically served life is less and less acceptable to her. Finally, she begins to weep and cannot stop.

Then a wonderful moment occurs; the native wisdom of the daughter, which is so deep that no one can deprive her of it, comes to the surface and prescribes its specific cure for her feminine wound. She goes alone to the forest.

Feminine wounds are almost always cured by being still. A man, or the masculine side of a woman, generally has to take an outwardly heroic stance with his problems. Our mythology is full of the heroic man who mounts his white horse and goes galloping off to do the heroic deed, which is his way of addressing the wrongs of life. We are all aware of the masculine ideal of heroism which has been ingrained in us from the medieval world to our own times—from the knights of King Arthur's Round Table to Star Trek. But woman's genius is quite the reverse. When a woman is aware of her problem, the healing comes spontaneously and from the depths of her nature. Solitude is the feminine equivalent of masculine heroic action.

The masculine heroic task is to take sword and lance in hand and charge with all power at the enemy. The enemy is so dark and so thoroughly identified with evil that there is never any question about his satanic character. Almost all of our patriarchal culture is based on this dichotomy of good and evil. For a medieval mind there is nothing so thrilling as to recognize evil, lower visor and lance, and charge at it with all one's energy and power. To fight for the good against the evil is the essence of man's heroic nature.

But the medieval mind is diminishing in the presence of modern consciousness and particularly in its impact with modern science.

Woman's heroic way is based on an entirely different view of reality. When the feminine is faced with a conflict, it is her nature to search out the opposing forces that have collided and put an end to the illusory battle between them. A man wants to ensure the triumph of good over evil; a woman wants to diminish the opposition between the two. He fights; she reconciles. More accurately, these are the masculine and feminine ways whether they are found in a man or in a woman.

John Sanford tells a story from medieval times that is to the point: The theologians of the time were in great distress at a dilemma they could not solve with their sharp masculine discrimination. It seems that a very nearsighted priest had seen a flock of penguins on a trip far into the southern regions and, thinking they were people because of his faulty vision, had given them a blessing. Because of the blessings were the penguins given souls? Insoluble dilemma! A schism was threatening over such a major issue but no one could find a just solution. Someone thought to take the issue to St. Theresa, who immediately found a workable solution. "Give them souls," she replied, "but little ones." The feminine capacity for finding a way between conflicting opposites has a heroic quality about it that eluded the black-and-white thinking of the theologians.

The handless maiden listens to her innermost wisdom, goes to the woods, and is quiet. There is immediate relief in this since it is less lonely to be alone than to be in false relationships. She is hungry, scratched by the briars, helpless without hands to serve herself. But she is at home in her feminine world of the forest. Here is the native power of inner femininity.

FINDING THE KING'S GARDEN

By chance—except that there is no chance in the mythological world—the maiden blunders into a garden. Any woman who exercises her feminine genius of stillness will find her way to the garden, that most feminine of all symbols, the center of her being. More than this, it is the king's garden; she has found her way to the Self, that center which exists outside of time and space and is not wounded by any human mischance.

81

She has to pass over a bog or swamp on the way to the king's garden, and this represents the difficulty of the solitary journey. This passage is not assured and many die of despair on the way. A woman must keep faith and endure or she will disappear in the solitary swamp. Our handless maiden does endure and with the aid of an angel from heaven she finds herself in the king's garden.

In the garden is a pear tree, much prized by the king, with every pear labeled and numbered. What a wonderful symbol of the patriarchal world, where everything is cataloged and numbered! The masculine mentality that lives such an ordered life would reply, if you questioned him, that one cannot run a kingdom on any other basis. True; but at what mechanical cost?

The handless maiden is very hungry from her solitary wanderings in the swamp, the more so since she has had no hands to aid her. She manages to eat one of the pears without aid of hands and thus, life is possible for her. Pears? What lies behind this odd symbol? If the apple wounded us in the Garden of Eden, is this the redemption of that wound by something very similar but just enough different to be curative? The pear has long been a symbol of the Virgin Mary and is a very feminine form. Since it was a masculine act (by the devil

82

and the miller) that cost the maiden her hands, it is understandable that a very feminine object would bring about the healing of that act. The maiden eats one pear a day and in this manner survives.

The king's gardener notices that one pear a day is disappearing and reports this to the king. The monarch, being a kind and just man, waits in hiding with his gardener to see what is happening to his beloved pears. The two see the pathetic sight of the handless maiden coming early in the morning for her single pear of the day; the king falls instantly in love with her. It is often the fate of a woman who is to be the consort of a king to have great difficulty in lesser relationships. All the suffering of the handless maiden comes into focus now and we begin to see that all the bad fortune has been the device by which the maiden could meet with the king. This is to say that one's life sometimes goes very badly on a personal level so that one is driven to a deeper level where the very best may occur.

What a wonderful progression of events! The fateful wound given to the handless maiden from an uncomprehending masculine source has been eased by the same fateful quality in a feminine way. If a wounded woman can keep faith in the feminine curative power to be found in solitude, she will, as if by a miracle, find her way to a feminine healing. This seems foreign to our modern patriarchal way of thinking, but it is the one cure that can redeem the masculine wound in a woman. No masculine devices have the slightest effect on this specific kind of wound.

SILVER HANDS, THE KING'S GIFT

The king takes the handless maiden home with him and makes her his queen. She implores him that she could not possibly be queen without hands. He assures her that she will have everything done for her and she will need no hands. Here is that masculine logic that is so difficult to refute! The masculine voice of reality offers the same argument all over again! Even though it comes from the king this time, it is the same masculine logic.

But it is very awkward to have a queen without hands. True, she has servants and needs do no work, but certain graceful feminine things required of a queen cannot be managed without hands. So the king calls his magicians and orders them to prepare silver hands to be fitted to the handless arms; and the new queen is presented to the court with her silver hands.

She is the delight of the court, and her lovely silver-handed ways are the talk of the whole kingdom.

Silver hands? What has this generous, gentle king done now? He unwittingly provided the pears that saved the life of the handless maiden, and now he provides silver hands, makes her respectable and famous for her silvery grace. But note that one gift was natural, the other artificial. Does it follow that a masculine solution to a feminine problem is always artificial, or worse, more trickery? This is certainly the most refined trickery yet! Is it an echo of the fact that it was masculine trickery that cost the maiden her hands in the first place? Now there is more masculine trickery represented by the magicians who attempt a repair. But it is only an artificial repair, even though it works well for a time.

It is not an admirable trait in men that they will convince women that silver-handedness is a high virtue. A man is often only too ready to keep a woman in the silver-handed state, as long as it is the man who determines the character of the silver hands. One hears of a gilded cage—which is still a cage no matter how golden it might be. This is another example of domination, which is sterling silver—but nonetheless an artificial existence for the woman.

It is the artificiality that is the terrible note in this part of our story. Almost without exception, a handless maiden has recourse to artificial femininity to replace the loss of her natural femininity. She learns the manners, customs, and gracefulness of acquired femininity, which are as brittle and metallic as the silver tea set over which she presides. And for a time even she is pleased with this. Her whole kingdom pays her compliments and tribute for her silver-handed gracefulness, which makes such a good substitute for human flesh-and-blood femininity. An artificial function is often more prized than the natural one. But it is only a substitute and carries no human value.

So much of our manners, training, and gracefulness is silver-handed. Often it is the feminine currency for a whole society. We think we are getting by with this manner of relatedness until we awaken to the terrible hunger and loneliness that result from silver-handedness. No other loneliness is as deep as silver-handedness. It is the worst, since it is covered over so well with an artificial value, more highly prized than human qualities.

I was lecturing on this story once at a conference in one of the finest hotels in America. Having just talked about silver-handedness, I began watching in this aristocratic setting for that silver-handed quality. Nowhere

86

in America have I been served more carefully. But all of the service was of the most exquisitely wrought silver! It came straight from a training school that prepares all of its graduates to serve with silver hands—sterling silver in this case. All, that is, except for a big Irish lad who made human contact with me over the breakfast table. He was too genuine to have absorbed the schooling! His use of real hands gave me permission to use my own hands, and we had a warm human exchange. Most exchanges preceding that during the weekend had been carefully crafted of silver—both in people around me and in myself. Fresh from discussing this subject, I consciously found the difference between silver and human hands in that great hotel. I had been unconsciously aware of this difference all of my life—as is everybody else—but it took the best possible silver to show the unmistakable difference between silver and human hands.

The first effect that one sees from a silver-handed atmosphere is that it is terribly isolating. To be touched in this way is to be isolated; one unconsciously replies in the same mechanical, unrelated, and metallic way. Silver hands are the death of any feminine aspect of relationship. Metal is never an adequate substitute for humanness. Even at its best, silver is cold.

A story by Ray Bradbury, told and retold and finally surfacing in altered form as told by a storyteller in India, relates the awful result of silver-handedness: It is the year 2500, with robotics developed to a fine art. A woman wishes to bail out of her marriage but not hurt her spouse. Robotics offers a way through this dilemma. She has a robot of herself made and intends to substitute it for herself without her husband knowing it. At the last moment one small difficulty arises; it seems that humans have a heartbeat but robots give off a 60-cycle hum. She programs the robot to record the husband's heartbeat as its first act and incorporate this into itself. Then there will be no chance that the husband will ever know. The robot is introduced into the marriage; it goes to the husband to take the necessary recording of the heartbeat—and finds a 60-cycle hum in the husband! This is a terrible story of the silver-hands mentality carried to its ultimate extreme.

WEEPING AND REENTERING THE FOREST

The queen has a baby boy in due time, and with all the servants to care for it everything goes well. But unaccountably, the queen begins to weep one day and cannot stop her tears. She wants to take care of her own baby with her own hands. The king, in his inimitable masculine logic, tries to convince her that there is no need for her to do anything since it can all be done by the servants. But this time his logic does not prevail and the tears come without stopping.

There is a historical parallel to this, at first amusing but unendurably sad upon reflection. Marie Antoinette, queen of Louis the XVI, became aware of the silver-handed life she was living. Probably no more stilted or mannered life had ever been lived than in the courts of the French monarchy, and the poor queen was caught in an endless round of artificiality. Beauty, grace, dignity, and wealth were everywhere; but all this was at the expense of ordinary earthy humanness. Marie Antoinette decided to import something peasantlike and earthy into her life, so she ordered a cow barn to be built at Versailles. The best architects of the realm were engaged and a masterpiece was constructed. The exquisite barn can still be seen at Versailles. The finest cows were imported from Switzerland and the queen went with her ladies-in-waiting to do the first milking. This was to be her touch with earthy femininity. At the last moment she decided that this was far too messy an endeavor and instructed her servants to do the milking.

The queen had come very close to challenging her sterling existence; but at the last moment she lost her inspiration and only added another bit of silver to her environment. Who knows? Perhaps the tragic course of the French monarchy might have been altered if the queen had consented to milk a cow. If the feminine principle can keep its earth (hand) connection, the stratospheric excesses of the masculine and the patriarchal world might be averted. In England our term *grounded* (as used in electrical terminology) is expressed as *earthed*. Both are eloquent.

Tears are a wonderful way of reverting to a simpler realm and gaining a new chance at a failed mission. We surround ourselves with the salt ocean from which we originally sprang and are refreshed by that salty world.

The queen weeps her salt tears and cannot be consoled by all the compliments and servants and well-wishers that surround her. Silver hands will never provide relationship, and every woman knows this from her deep feminine instinct. Whole kingdoms may thrive on the artificiality of silver hands, but no real woman will be content with this. So the queen washes away an unworkable way of life with her tears. She exercises her feminine wisdom, the instinct that is in every woman, and she takes her son to the solitude of the forest. Just as she had saved herself from her destructive father earlier in the story, now she saves herself from the more subtle but not less dangerous domination of the king.

It is not easy at first glance to see that the danger from the king is not less for a woman than the danger from the father. The king has been so kind and has raised the handless maiden from her wandering and given her so much, the highest gift being the silver hands. But these gifts are no less dangerous to her than the wound that her father gave her by his bargain with the devil. To be trapped in silver-handedness is no less isolating than to be incapacitated by having one's hands chopped off. If anything, it is worse, since it is not as obvious. Many women are trapped in their sterling silver way of life and never know that this is the cause of their weeping.

I remember a movie long years ago with a scene of a robber holding up a couple in their Cadillac in the desert. It is the meeting of a rough world with a silvery world. The woman awakens to the fact that she has lived as a prisoner in her Cadillac existence and suddenly she begs the robber to take her off into his world. She wants to exchange silver hands for his bohemian existence. Of course this will only be jumping from the frying pan into the fire and will be no solution at all. But the film portrays with genius the moment of her awakening to her silver-handed existence. Cadillacs suddenly seem vastly inferior to the rough—but real—world that has intruded into her life. Many people never wake up to the sterility of their sterling existence. This is most often the experience of a woman, but it can be as powerful for the interior feminine values of a man.

When a man awakens to the silver hands of his interior feminine, his feeling function, it is similar to a woman's experience. He has learned his particular devil's bargain of feeling—saying and doing all the right things, roses at anniversaries, clever phrases, infinite promises that dazzle a woman, all the genteel things of class and aristocracy. All of these things are true and valuable, but not if they are given by silver hands. If he continues to develop, one day he realizes he has been giving silver-handed products from his feeling nature and has been cheating everyone around him! It is a painful moment when one realizes he has been giving a mechanical product to his world and that there is little real feeling in it. The interior feminine in a man must then go through a process very similar to the woman's to heal his artificiality of feeling.

The queen has instinctively understood that aloneness is better than false relationship—even if it be of sterling silver—and she takes refuge in that greatest of all feminine healers—solitude. She lives with her baby in the woods and exists on the simplest possible fare. Nothing happens, which is enough to frighten any modern person. But that kind of nothingness is the accumulation or storing of healing energy.

The king is frantic at losing her, for he truly loves his queen; but his love is too one-sided and has been a prison for her, albeit a sterling prison.

It is genius to store energy. Though one has no idea what that energy will be used for, to have a store of energy accumulated is to have power in back of one. We live with our psychic energy in modern times much as we do with our money—mortgaged into the next decade. Most modern people are exhausted nearly all the time and never catch up to an equilibrium of energy, let alone have a store of energy behind them. With no energy in store, one cannot meet any new opportunity.

As soon as the queen has bathed herself in the restorative salt bath of tears and gathered a reserve of energy, a most wonderful thing happens. The miracle begins as an emergency—as so many wonderful things do—when her baby falls into a stream and will drown if not rescued immediately. The queen cries for her servants to help—for she has been indoctrinated into her silver-hands mentality to this degree—but of course no servant is there. Then in a sublime moment of strength (perhaps thanks to the stored energy?), she plunges her useless silver hands into the stream to rescue her child. When she draws the child from the water, miracle!— the baby is safe and her hands are completely restored to flesh and blood.

What a wonderful moment! What a sublime healing! Was it the plunging of her hands into the healing water that effected the cure—much as the tears had been the healing before? Or was it simply the passage of time and the long, painful process of the solitude that had healed her? Or was it the sudden eruption of love and devotion to her child? In any case, the healing is a marvel of interior evolution and the faith of a woman capable of following her own feminine way.

The New Femininity

Our story is acute in providing a diagnosis and prescription for a dark drama that most modern women suffer in our enlightened times. The patriarchal world

94

has produced for us the highest standard of living ever known, mechanical wonders, and magic unknown to former generations, 747s, computers, telephones, television, global transport—things no king or emperor knew a century ago. But our story tells the cost of this bargain and gives some clue to the loneliness and subtle suffering that we carry with us. The curative solitude and the healing tears come automatically to us—for nature is aware of our suffering—but we do not put them in the right place or recognize their curative value. All symptoms are healing, but only if we listen to them and respond.

As with all stories and myths, the greatest value of the tale of the handless maiden is in its inner dimensions. Its wisdom applies to the masculine and feminine qualities deep inside ourselves, whether we be male or female. The handless maiden is as important to a man's inner feminine as it is to a woman's primary character. The tears are not necessarily an outpouring of visible tears but may be that subtle ache deep inside either a man or a woman. Entering the forest is not necessarily a dramatic leaving of a marriage or a flamboyant outer move; it may best be done by a change in attitude or a quiet experiment in one's life that would not be noticed immediately by an outer observer.

It is healing for any person to hear the priceless heritage of our stories and find a contemporary translation of their prescriptions applicable to his or her immediate circumstances.

CONCLUSION

SINCE OUR TWO MYTHS ARE from early times, they speak of what was to come in our society. They give an accurate forecast; it takes no genius to see the wound-edness of both man and woman in our present society. Few men escape the fisher king wound; it is perhaps the most persistent ailment of our time. Women are angry about their status in modern society and are struggling to find terms for their suffering.

What is the prospect for this evolution of conscious-ness? That rare product of civilization—conscious-ness—seems always to be the outcome of suffering. What is evolving out of this particular form of suffering?

The first task is to take the suffering inside as an interior event. As long as one blames someone outside or holds some institution responsible for the problem, there is little chance of learning or enhancing consciousness.

If a man can find the Parsifal inside himself, take responsibility for it, and weave that evolutionary process into his conscious life, he can find his way to the Grail castle. After all, it is only down the road a little way, to the left, and across the drawbridge. . . . His chief duty is to ask the necessary question. I take great encouragement from the fact that he need only ask the question; he does not have to be wise or powerful enough to answer it.

Likewise, a woman who finds herself caught up in the drama of a devil's bargain—personal or cultural—can find her feminine way through the forest of solitude and discover her own genuine humanity.

Such a person—man or woman—will have some specific characteristics. He or she will have a genuine feeling structure of personality and inspire a similar response from anyone he or she meets. One knows immediately if a response from another person was just polite courtesy or whether it was heartfelt and a gift from the depth of that person. Such people are healers and leave a golden glow in their wake through even the most ordinary circumstances. A healed person is automatically a healer. And his or her strength is the greater for having been through dark times and having brought a conscious solution as a gift to the world.